The Root

of the Blues

by Peggy Bresnick Kendler

Scott Foresman
is an imprint of

Glenview, Illinois • Boston, Massachusetts • Chandler, Arizona
Upper Saddle River, New Jersey

ISBN 13: 978-0-328-52520-1
ISBN 10:   0-328-52520-0

West African Music

The blues is a style of music. It has been popular in the United States since its invention in the early 1900s. Its roots go back to the music of West Africa.

Music has always been important to the many cultures of West Africa. It is a part of life for even the youngest West African child. For centuries, West Africans have made music in many ways for all sorts of occasions.

In West Africa, music or dance is a part of many activities, such as working, playing, and celebrating. Songs are often sung accompanied by drums, or with stringed musical instruments similar to the guitar and banjo.

Blues has its roots in West African music.

West African Musical Traditions

West African music is unique. It combines sounds from nature with spoken words. Each sound and song has its own unique meaning to the African people.

People called *griots* played an important role in West African music. Griots were musical entertainers. They played instruments that looked and sounded similar to a banjo.

The griots traveled from village to village playing music, telling jokes and stories, and giving advice. They knew about the history of each village and explained it through songs and stories. People came to **appreciate** them for the advice and entertainment that they offered.

A West African banjo (left) and a North American banjo (right)

The music that would become the blues developed among enslaved African Americans.

Coming to America

The English colony of Virginia was started in 1607. The first shipment of enslaved people arrived in 1619. This date marks the true beginning of the history of the blues.

The enslaved people were West Africans. They had been captured from their villages and forced onto ships bound for the Americas. Once the West Africans arrived, plantation owners purchased them from the people who brought them over. The West Africans were given just food, water, and shelter, but they were not paid for their work. And they were not free to leave. Living in **slavery** was very hard.

A Life of Slavery

Between 1619 and 1808, millions of enslaved West Africans were brought by ship to the Americas. Among them were West Africans who had once been griots. Instead of telling jokes and stories as they would have back in West Africa, these former griots sang songs that told of their unhappiness and expressed their fear that they would never see their homes again.

Most enslaved people did farm labor on plantations. They often sang work songs while working in the fields.

These songs often focused on their sadness. But they also kept the enslaved West Africans' spirits up as they worked. Enslaved people managed to preserve the unique West African musical style through their work songs.

While laboring in the fields, they used a West African musical technique called *call-and-response*. The song leader would call out a sentence or phrase. Then the other people would sing with an answering sentence or phrase, as a **choir** in a church might do.

Call-and-response was a kind of musical conversation. One person led, and the others followed. The enslaved people also sang *field hollers*. These were long, drawn-out cries sung over long distances, from one field to the next.

A modern choir

Early African Americans sang spirituals, songs that reflected their hopes for the future.

Religion Shapes Music

Many of the enslaved West Africans were introduced to Christianity after they were brought to the Americas. They continued to celebrate their own West African traditions, but they also practiced some parts of Christianity. The parts that spoke about freedom from suffering were especially popular.

The plantation owners forbade their enslaved workers from meeting in groups, so they met secretly. During those secret meetings they prayed, danced, and spoke of their own personal experiences. They also sang a type of song called a *spiritual.*

Spirituals were both **religious** and full of emotion. They expressed the enslaved West Africans' feelings and hopes for the future. Spirituals played an important role in the development of blues music.

The Blues Comes of Age

No one knows where the first blues song was performed, or who sang or wrote it. What we do know, however, is that blues music sprang up in different parts of the American South during the 1890s.

Early blues music was inspired by call-and-response, field hollers, and spirituals. The earliest blues singers played handmade musical instruments, which made interesting and unusual sounds.

The Roots of Blues Music

1912 An early blues song, W. C. Handy's "Memphis Blues" is published.

1914 W. C. Handy's "St. Louis Blues" is published.

1920 Mamie Smith records "Crazy Blues."

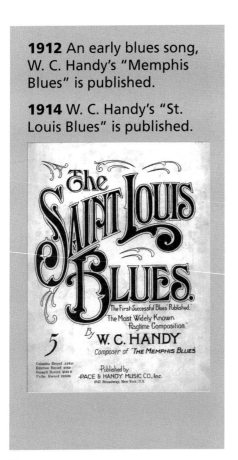

Among these early instruments were the handmade banjo, and the washboard and stick. Later on, blues musicians would play guitars, pianos, and harmonicas. Blues musicians became known for experimenting with different sounds.

Early blues music was usually played by roaming musicians who were similar to the griots. Their audiences were mostly farm workers who would take breaks from their work and dance to the music.

1923 Bessie Smith records "Down Hearted Blues." Gertrude "Ma" Rainey records "New Boweavil Blues." The recordings help make blues popular throughout the United States.

1925–1929 "Blind Lemon" Jefferson records nearly one hundred blues songs.

1930s Different types of blues music begin to appear in different areas, such as the Mississippi delta and Memphis, Tennessee.

Early blues musician W. C. Handy is sometimes called "the Father of the Blues."

Early Blues Musicians

In 1903, W. C. Handy heard a man in the Tutwiler, Mississippi, train station playing the guitar. The man slid a pocket knife up and down the guitar, making an unusual sound.

What Handy heard was an early form of the slide guitar blues. Later, he wrote down the notes. Blues historians believe this was the first time that blues music was written down.

Handy later gained fame as a bandleader, songwriter, and performer. He published "Memphis Blues," an early blues song, in 1912.

Mamie Smith was a stage singer and the first person to record a blues song. Smith recorded "Crazy Blues" in 1920. Smith inspired other female singers to record blues music.

"Blind Lemon" Jefferson was a singer, musician, and songwriter. Jefferson, who was blind since childhood, recorded nearly one hundred blues songs from 1925 to 1929.

Bessie Smith was an early blues singer. She wrote many blues songs, including the hit, "Back Water Blues." She also influenced many future female blues singers.

Gertrude "Ma" Rainey is sometimes called "the Mother of the Blues." She began singing blues on stage in 1904 and recorded blues music in 1923.

Different Places, Different Styles

Slavery was abolished in 1865. Formerly enslaved people were **released** to settle anywhere in the country. Different styles of blues were created as they moved around.

The Memphis Blues, which originated in Memphis, Tennessee, featured one guitarist playing rhythm guitar and another one playing lead guitar. The East Texas Blues sounded like old work songs. It used guitar or piano for rhythm. The Piedmont Blues, from North Carolina, was influenced by ragtime, a form of jazz music. It was more melodic than other blues styles.

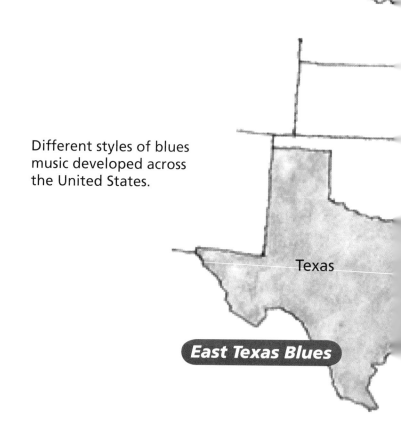

Different styles of blues music developed across the United States.

Texas

East Texas Blues

The Delta Blues began among African Americans of the Mississippi Delta. It blended work songs and field hollers with musicians playing slide guitars and harmonicas. In Chicago, blues musicians added electric guitar and drums to the Delta Blues style. Their music became known as Chicago Blues.

Chicago Blues

Illinois

West Virginia

Virginia

Memphis Blues

Piedmont Blues

North Carolina

Delta Blues

South Carolina

Georgia

Tennessee

Mississippi

Louisiana

Arkansas

Modern Blues Greats

There have been hundreds of great blues musicians since the early 1900s. Millions of listeners have enjoyed their music.

The most famous blues musicians each have their own style and talent. For example, Bo Diddley's soul music influenced rock and roll. Billie Holiday was a world-famous female vocalist. Her soulful style of singing the blues was unique and personalized. John Lee Hooker's growling voice blended with one repeating musical chord for a special blues style.

Bo Diddley

Muddy Waters

B. B. King, who grew up in Mississippi and lived in Memphis, Tennessee, as a **teenager** and young man, has been called "the King of the Blues." King often picks at a single guitar string to produce many different emotional sounds. As a boy, Muddy Waters worked in the cotton fields of the Mississippi delta. In the early 1940s, he moved to Chicago to play the blues. Waters eventually became one of the great Chicago Blues musicians.

John Lee Hooker

Billie Holiday

B. B. King

The blues is related to many forms of popular music, including the jazz that is being played by these musicians.

The Blues and Its Relatives

Blues music has had a major influence on today's popular music. You can find elements of the blues in most of the modern popular music styles, including jazz, rock, rap, and soul.

Buddy Bolden formed one of the first jazz bands in 1895. Buddy, who may have started out working as a **barber,** played the cornet, an instrument similar to a bugle or trumpet. His jazz music sounded a great deal like the blues music of the time.

One of today's popular musical styles, rap, comes from the same roots as the blues. Rap has rhyming lyrics. The lyrics are spoken rhythmically while musical instruments are played. Rap music often tells stories in a style similar to that used by the griots.

Without the blues, American music would be very different from what it is today. From its quiet beginnings, the blues has become a major part of American life!

Glossary

appreciate *v.* to think highly of; to recognize the worth or quality of; value; enjoy

barber *n.* a person whose business is cutting hair and shaving or trimming beards

choir *n.* a group of singers who sing together, often in a church service

released *v.* let go, freed, unlatched

religious *adj.* much interested in the belief, study, and worship of God or gods; devoted to religion

slavery *n.* the condition of being owned by another person and being made to work without wages

teenager *n.* a person between the ages of thirteen and nineteen

Surviving the Elements:
Animals in Their Environments

by Joe Adair

Scott Foresman
is an imprint of

Glenview, Illinois • Boston, Massachusetts • Chandler, Arizona
Upper Saddle River, New Jersey

ISBN 13: 978-0-328-52529-4
ISBN 10:   0-328-52529-4

7 8 9 10 V0FL 16 15 14 13

CONTENTS

Think of animals you have seen at the zoo or on TV. Maybe you have pets. How many kinds of animals do you think share our planet? There are too many to count. They come in all shapes, colors, and sizes.

Animals have grown and adapted in many different ways to survive. They grow and **specialize**, or change, very slowly. Even the smallest change can take thousands of years. These changes make animals more successful at finding food, running fast, hiding from enemies, and other survival skills.

In the pages that follow you will find out about these animal changes. You will also read about different kinds of habitats, or animal homes.

You probably know what a giraffe looks like. They have really long necks! This makes it possible for them to reach the leaves way up on the treetops. That is how they have adapted to survive. Now, let's read about other remarkable animals and their homes!

Maybe you have seen a polar bear. They are huge white bears that love to swim in icy water. They don't get cold, though. Why? Because they have adapted to survive in the frigid Arctic weather. Polar bears have a thick coat of fur and a layer of fat that **enables** them to keep warm.

Polar bears are great swimmers. They can swim for hours. They can also swim a very long way. They use their front paws to swim, just like dogs do. They keep their back legs flat to help them steer. They can also close their nostrils underwater.

Our planet has many different habitats. Some are very cold while others are very hot. Some habitats are wet, and some are very dry. The shape of the land is also important. A habitat may have mountains, rivers, or large flat areas covered with grass.

We are going to learn about six different kinds of habitats: the Arctic tundra, temperate forests, grasslands, deserts, tropical rain forests, and tide pools. Each of these habitats has very different animals.

Chapter One

Animals in the Arctic Tundra

We know that the Arctic is a very cold place. Can you think of animals that would live in very cold places? Only a few kinds of animals can live in such a cold place. The average temperature in the winter is –30°F and during the summer it ranges between 37°F and 54°F.

The Arctic tundra includes Greenland and the northern parts of Alaska, Canada, and Russia. Winters are very long and harsh, while summers are short and cool. During the summer, the sun shines all day and most of the night. During the winter, the sun is low and the sky is mostly dark.

There is a layer of ground that is frozen all year. This layer is called permafrost. Some people think that permafrost is **sterile** and that nothing can grow in the tundra. However, plants can grow there. In summer, the layer above the permafrost thaws, and plants with shallow roots can grow.

Most animals that live in the Arctic tundra use it as a summer home. Many birds and mammals migrate to this part of the world for the warmer summers. Other animals live here all year. It's amazing that any animal can survive here because food is hard to find and drinking water is often frozen.

One animal that has survived the harsh cold is the musk ox. It has thick fur to shield it from the cold. It's like a built-in winter coat! The musk ox actually has two coats of fur. One is long, and the other is short. Both coats are **critical**. These coats work together to trap warm air between them.

The large and powerful hooves of the musk ox are good tools for breaking ice. These hooves enable the musk ox to drink the water underneath the ice.

musk ox

Besides the polar bear, the brown bear also lives in the Arctic tundra. This bear has adapted to the cold by hibernating. This means that the bear sleeps right through most of the freezing winter.

In the summer, the brown bear eats just about everything in sight! It stores this food in its body for the long winter sleep. The food becomes a layer of fat to keep the bear warm and fed during hibernation.

Chapter Two

Animals in Temperate Forests

You are probably familiar with temperate forest areas. Temperate forests are found in eastern North America, Western Europe, and Eastern Asia.

In these forests, the trees lose their leaves each fall. As temperatures drop, the leaves turn different colors and fall to the forest floor. There are four seasons in this region, just as you may be used to. Animals learn to live through each season.

Insects, birds, reptiles, and mammals have adapted well to these parts of the world. A squirrel is a common animal in temperate forests. Squirrels have adapted by learning to store food away. They hide their food in many places. It's stored away for the winter months when food is very **scarce**, or hard to find. The cold weather keeps these nuts and seeds fresh.

These woodland animals live in temperate forests.

Raccoons live in temperate forests.

Raccoons also live in temperate forests. They are one of the most adaptable creatures in the forest. They have thick fur and little front paws that look like hands. Their claws are sharp so they can climb trees. They can open all sorts of containers to get food that people throw away as garbage. They eat nuts, fruit, fish, small animals, frogs, and even candy! These animals sleep in the daytime and roam around at night.

Chapter Three

Animals in Grasslands

The region we will learn about now is the grassland. We will focus on a special type of grassland called a savanna. In savannas, temperatures are much warmer. The largest savannas are found in Africa. Other grasslands can be found in North America and South America. The African savannas are home to lions, zebras, and elephants. Savannas have tall grasses and very few trees. There are two main seasons in the savanna, wet and dry. The wet season is usually in summer, while winter is the dry season. The dry season is often when great fires burn. These fires keep the savanna open and grassy.

■ Grasslands of the world

■ Savannahs

Elephants graze in the savanna.

During the dry season water is hard to find. For this reason, some animals are forced to migrate to places where water is more plentiful. The elephant has a way to get water from places that no other animal can reach. This water is stored in the trunks of Boabab trees. The elephant is large and strong enough to rip open the tree trunk to get to the water. Once the tree is opened, the elephant uses its trunk to suck out the water.

Elephants rest during the warm part of the day and once or twice more at night. They usually move slowly about the savannas as they search for food. A healthy elephant grows so large that it has no enemies to threaten it as it searches for food and water. Elephants weigh up to 7 tons and can eat up to 440 pounds of plants and vegetation a day!

The lion is another animal of the savanna. These cats are large and very strong. The male lions are larger than the female lions and have large manes around their heads.

Lions also live in groups called prides. Living in prides is an example of adaptation. A pride of lions can work together hunting and defending the area where the family lives. Many times they are defending this area from other lions. Lions spend about 20 hours a day resting! They hunt during the day for animals such as zebras, gazelles, and buffaloes.

Chapter Four

Animals in Hot Deserts

Deserts get only a small amount of precipitation, making this a very dry climate. There are hot and cold deserts. We're going to read about hot deserts. The temperatures in a desert can change from very hot during the day to very cold at night. Deserts are very hard to live in because of the lack of water and the great temperature changes.

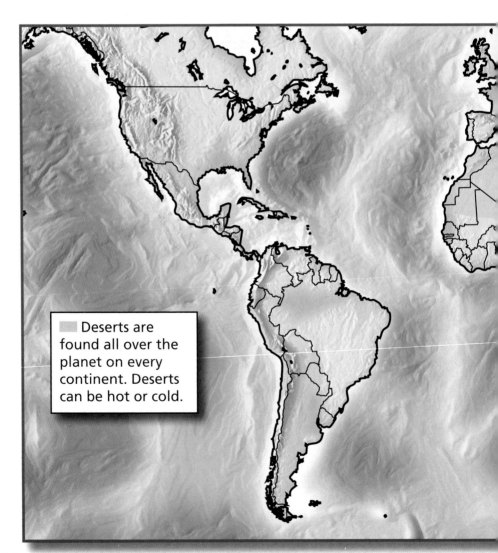

Deserts are found all over the planet on every continent. Deserts can be hot or cold.

Desert animals have ways to keep cool. Birds, reptiles, and small mammals are adapted to life in the desert. The black-tailed Jack Rabbit is one animal that can survive in the desert. This rabbit has a black stripe on its tail. Black-tailed Jack Rabbits spend most of the day in the shade. They rest until it is cool enough to go out and find food. Staying out of the sun helps them keep more of the water that is already in their bodies.

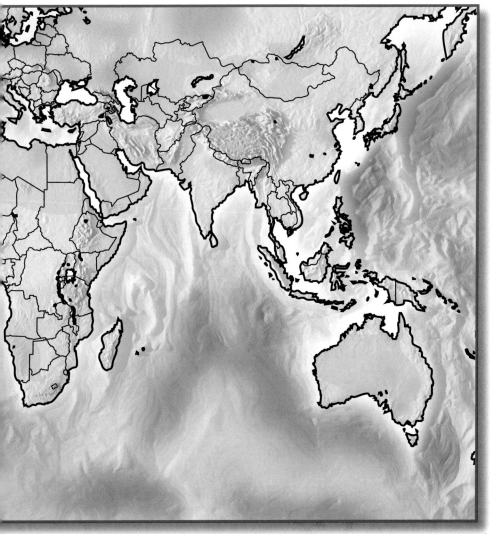

Sidewinder snakes move sideways across the sand.

The sidewinder is a snake that lives in the desert. These snakes move very quickly over the sand and rock of deserts. They move in a side-to-side motion. These snakes eat lizards, small mice, and sometimes birds. This desert snake hunts at night. During the day it stays in the holes of other animals or finds shade under bushes.

Dingoes are found in the deserts of Australia. Dingoes have adapted by hunting kangaroos and small rabbits. Deserts are difficult places to live. Animals can adapt to anyplace on earth, even the most difficult places.

Chapter Five

Animals in Tropical Rain Forests

Unlike deserts, tropical rain forests are very moist. They get from 60 to 160 inches of rain each year! Tropical rain forests have more different kinds of life than any other region on Earth. There are millions of plants and animals in these warm, wet regions. Animals in rain forests have plenty of water to drink and plants to eat. The trees in rain forests are very tall, green, and thick. Monkeys, snakes, birds, and lizards live in these trees. Some of the animals that live in the trees never even touch the ground! They are adapted to stay away from larger animals on the ground that would hunt them. Life in the trees provides all that they need to live.

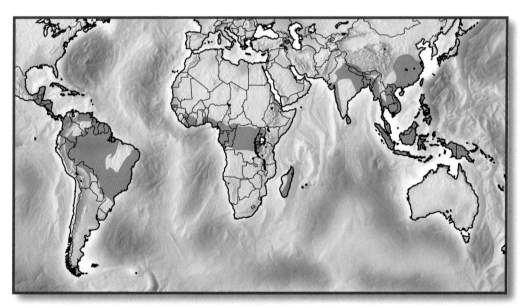

Rain forests around the world

A toucan is a large, colorful rain forest bird. It has a very large beak. This beak is an adaptation that helps it eat the food it needs to survive. There are so many animals in

A tropical bird, the toucan

the rain forest that there is great competition for food. Animals like the toucan have adapted in their own way to survive. Their long beaks let them reach berries growing on high branches. When they have a berry in their giant beaks, they often toss the food to their neighbors.

You may not think of pigs as tropical animals but they are. The bearded pig is a tropical animal that follows birds, like toucans, from the ground. They catch any pieces of fruit the birds may drop. They have long snouts used to churn up the earth. There they find their food: roots, earthworms, fruit, and seeds.

Chapter Six

Animals in Tide Pools

Tide pools form where sea water is trapped in rocky hollows. Most of the animals that live in these tide pools are invertebrates, which means that they do not have backbones. The tide pool protects them from being hurt by the crashing waves or being eaten by other animals. Tide pools also contain coral. Coral has adapted by using **mucus** to capture food it needs to live.

Starfish, or sea stars, can also grow their limbs back. They are found in different levels of tide pools. They can wrap around rocks to catch food. In fact, they can cling so tightly to rocks that the powerful tide cannot wash them away.

Glossary

critical *adj.* very important; urgent

enables *v.* makes possible; gives something the power or material it needs to do a specific task

mucus *n.* a slippery substance that comes from the body of an animal

scarce *adj.* difficult to find

specialize *v.* to adapt or change for a habitat

sterile *adj.* unable to create food or life